Revolting
REMEDIES
from the Middle Ages

Edited by Daniel Wakelin

and compiled by students of the University of Oxford

Bodleian Library
UNIVERSITY OF OXFORD

First published in 2018 by the Bodleian Library
Broad Street, Oxford OX1 3BG

www.bodleianshop.co.uk

ISBN 978 1 85124 476 8

Cover design by Dot Little at the Bodleian Library
Designed and typeset by Laura Parker, Paul Holberton Publishing,
in Hoefler Historial FellType and Lexicon No1 font
Printed and bound in China by C&C Offset Printing Co. Ltd on 100gsm
Chinese GS woodfree (Golden Sun)

British Library Catalogue in Publishing Data
A CIP record of this publication is available from the British Library

CONTENTS

INTRODUCTION

Here bygynneth gode medecyns for alle manere evel.

'Here begin good medicines for all manner of evils.'
So begins one set of cures for diseases starting
'For the hed' and running down to the toes,
from a manuscript in the Bodleian Library in
Oxford. From that and similar manuscripts,
we've collected a set of medical remedies from
the fifteenth century, the 1400s. There are
embarrassing ailments and painful procedures,
icky ingredients and bizarre beliefs. The would-be
doctors seem oblivious to pain, and any animal,
vegetable or mineral, let alone bodily fluid, can be
ground up, smeared on or inserted for medicinal
benefit. To be fair, these remedies open our eyes
to the resourcefulness and inventiveness of
generations past, evident in these homespun
household tips and the hands-on skill they rely
on. But nobody who has benefited from the
medicine of the twenty-first century would prefer

to endure eye-watering or eye-popping cures from the fifteenth.

So these remedies come with a health warning: *don't try this at home*. Those of us who have gathered these tips do not endorse them. You will not fix incontinence by sitting naked in a vat of ale. You will not stop your own wounds bleeding by slaying a pig. Nor do we condone the things done to other people or animals in these remedies. Please do not shave the skin off your feet to make a woman love you against her will: this is immoral. Please do not slit owls open to cure your gout: this is cruel.

A second warning is historical. The remedies in this book were not chosen to be typical of the medicine of their day but were chosen because they were funny or freaky in some way. If you were to read these remedies in the original manuscripts, you'd find them alongside hundreds more which use ordinary ingredients for realistic goals, such as soothing a headache with verbena or an upset stomach with fennel – cures which would not look out of place in a health-food shop today. Historians have shown that people in past generations made remedies which were often quite skilled, sensible and effective, as far as they could be by the knowledge of the time. Even in the stranger remedies collected here are many ingredients which would have worked: honey, verdigris, cobwebs and snail slime do all prevent or heal infection in some way. (Chapter six of Toni Mount's book *Medieval Medicine: Its Mysteries and Science* gives examples.) But we confess: for our book we chose the cures which seem weird and wonderful.

Often what make them seem odd are people's different sets of boundaries or limits. The techniques show blurred lines between medicine, magic and religion. There are different levels of squeamishness about bodily fluids and different levels of what psychotherapists call 'abjection'. There are different limits to the pain a doctor can expect a patient to endure, or that they will cause to animals. There is less firm a divide between humans and animals, so that what happens to one is affected by what happens to the other. There are few barriers between the human body and the objects one might put on it or into it. These funny or strange remedies reveal the different ways that people understood their world in the past.

Moreover, in the manuscripts, nor are these odd ones distinguished from those we would consider quite sane, such as herbal remedies; they are part of the same body of everyday wisdom. (Just a few remedies which involve magic are crossed out or noted by early readers as not permitted for Christians.) These things which seem odd to us were totally integrated into the mindset of the age.

The age from which these remedies come is the fifteenth century, give or take a few decades. This is the age in which increasingly many people learned to write and make books for themselves – copying by hand until and still after the coming of printing to England in 1476. They often copied out useful things such as medical remedies, as well as documents, religious teachings, grammar books and practical advice. Some of the remedies were gathered by doctors making books for themselves; others were gathered by laymen and women making notes of the practical medical tricks and techniques they had tried. A few collections were falsely ascribed to the great medical philosophers of antiquity, Hippocrates and Galen; some seem to be addressed to surgeons; but others seem to be folklore and common knowledge, passed from book to book and written down to remember them.

The remedies are mostly found in two places. Often single remedies are jotted on the flyleaves, margins or blank pages in books. The increasing number of literate people could not waste parchment or paper, which were expensive, so they wrote things to remember on the blank bits of other books. Other cures were gathered in collections, which were copied and recopied by others or plundered for single recipes in turn. Wherever they occur, remedies often have a short heading beginning 'For such-and-such a sickness'. This might be on a separate line, if there is room, or in larger or red letters, to let you quickly find the help you need. Sometimes, they end (as do remedies on pp. 100 and 104) with claims that the cure has been 'proved', or tried and tested, sometimes naming the medic, cleric or housewife who did it. It is still not clear how many remedies occur in multiple manuscripts. Sometimes, the same wording recurs from one book to another, but often the wording varies as scribes make slips unintendedly, or else choose to abbreviate or clarify what they copy. Even so, the same information might appear differently phrased in multiple jottings, suggesting that the ideas were passed on by word of mouth and in practice, as well as in books.

The language of these remedies in English, the everyday tongue, is more frank, less coolly scientific, than that of doctors today. It is simpler, too, than the artful poetry of Geoffrey Chaucer and his followers at that time. The people who wrote or rewrote remedies sought clarity and brevity. That said, the style is regular and patterned: 'Take A, do B and add C; and then mix D and E; also do F; and then you shall be well'. (They sometimes begin with the Latin word for *Take*: 'Recipe', whence our word *recipe* comes.) This is as conventional as the language of prayer – perhaps because both medicine and religion have elements of ritual – but these conventions are still familiar in the twenty-first century.

To make these remedies more readable, each one is here translated. Even translated, some names of diseases or of plants used as cures are rare in modern English. There are maladies such as *morphoea* and herbs such as *henbane*. Some plant names will be known to gardeners who remember the folklore of a couple of generations back; the translations tend to use these names and not the Latin jargon of botany. Many names for plants were checked in Tony Hunt's valuable dictionary *The Plant Names of Medieval England*. One ingredient remains a puzzle: 'a ded mannes hed' (p. 78) sounded like a very rare name for the dandelion, 'dedman flour' (Hunt, *Plant Names*, p. 99) but not exactly like it so it has been translated literally as a dead man's head.

Second, alongside the translations this book prints the remedies in the original fifteenth-century English. This book makes just a few changes: it replaces the fifteenth-century letterforms þ ('thorn') with our *th* and ȝ ('yogh') with our *g, gh* or *y*; it expands the abbreviations which people used to save effort and space; and it adjusts the letters *i, j, u* and *v*, the breaks between words and the punctuation to twenty-first-century conventions. It also silently corrects a few obvious slips of the pen by the scribes and removes a few later annotations.

The remedies were gathered by me and by various students who had taken my course for Oxford's Master's students in handling and reading manuscripts from the seventh to the sixteenth centuries. Seven students together submitted two thirds of the remedies printed here; I collected the rest and translated them all. (The students' contributions are listed at the back of the book by page.) The students often test their research skills on these medical manuscripts: the handwriting is a challenge, for these are practical notebooks, not fine works of calligraphy, and the technical terms test their knowledge of Middle English. But the students who sat in the library pained by this work often came back cured by laughter at the rude, revolting or remarkable remedies they found. We hope, now we've transcribed and translated them, that you will enjoy them as much as we did.

Daniel Wakelin

For to prefe qweder a seke man schall dy or lyfe

TAKE womans mylke of a knafe schylde, and if it be a woman, take the mylke of hyr as maydyn chylde, and the stalyng of the seke, and do the mylke to the seke uryn. And if it make a troute, he schall lyfe *et cetera — aliter non. Vel sic. Recipe* the uryne of the seke, and do it in a wessell and take womans mylke of a knafe chylde, and drope this over. And if it mell togyder, he schale lyfe, and if it flete abown, he is bott dede.

TO TEST WHETHER A SICK MAN SHALL DIE OR LIVE

Take the milk from a woman breastfeeding a baby boy, or if the sick person is a woman, take the milk from a woman who has a baby girl, and take the urine of the sick man, and add the milk to the diseased urine. If it coagulates, he shall live – otherwise not. *Or try this.* Take the urine of the sick man, and put it in a vessel, and take a woman's milk for a baby boy, and drip this over it. And if it mixes together, he shall live, and if it floats above, he's practically dead.

To geve a glestyr of the beste

Take and sette a schepys hedde, all to pecys, in a potell of watyr. Then put owt the fleche; put a hanfull mallows, marcwry, betyn, wylet levys, wormwod of hallf hanfull, a hanfull wette branne. Sethe to a quarte. Put in a sponfull of hony, the wayte of grote of sallte. Pute in to the bleddyr, a pynt at onys, and stop yt in.

HOW TO GIVE THE BEST ENEMA

Take a sheep's head, break it up into pieces
and put it in a pot of water. Then take out
the flesh; put in a handful of hollyhocks, the
herbs mercury and betony, violet leaves, half
a handful of wormwood, a handful of wheat
bran. Boil down to a quart of liquid. Put in
a spoonful of honey and salt that weighs as
much as a four pence piece. Squirt it into your
bladder, a pint at a time, and stopper it in there.

For the emerawdys

TAKE botyr and talwghe, bothe claryfied, and white oyle and alum icalcit, of all ylyche moche. Sette hem in a panne over a leuke fyre, til they been resolvyd. Than sette it doun and stere it, til it be colde. Anoynte hym that hath the emerawdys wyth this oynement, as far wythine the fundement as thou mayst, and then take a rostid oynoun and, as hoot as he may suffre, bynde it to his fundement. Serve hym thus ofte, and he schal be hole.

FOR HAEMORRHOIDS

Take butter and animal fat, both purified,
and white oil and a reduction of alum salt, the
same amount of each. Set them in a pan over
a lukewarm fire, until they're liquefied. Then
take it off the fire and stir it, until it's cold.
Anoint the man who has the haemorrhoids
with this ointment, as deep inside his bottom as
you can, and then take a roasted onion and, as
hot as he can bear, bind it to his bottom. Treat
him like this often, and he'll soon get better.

For goyng out of the foundement

Tak henne egges and seth tham in vynegre, and mell it with oyle of lorellmes, and sett thin ars theron oft tymes, till it be hole. *Another.* Tak poudre of herte horne and cast to thin ars. *Another.* Tak frankencence and seth it in water, and wesche the sore therwith, and late the breth go vp in to the foundement.

FOR A LEAKY BOTTOM

Take hens' eggs and boil them in vinegar, and mix it with oil of laurels, and sit your arse in it many times, until it's healed. *Another.* Take powder of a hart's horn and put it up your arse. *Another.* Take frankincense and boil it in water, and wash the sore with it, and let the steam from it go up your bottom.

Medicine for a man that is costyf

Tak and roste oynones, and ley to his navele, ymenged with may botre; and make hym wortes of hockes and of stanmarche, percilie of violet; and gyf hym ete therwith sour bred, and drynke smal ale; and gyf hym a subposotorie of a talwe candele in hys fundement. And so use it, for thou be hol.

MEDICINE FOR A MAN WHO IS CONSTIPATED

Take and roast onions, and lay them on his navel, mixed with unsalted butter; and make him a vegetable stew made of mallow plants, horse parsley and parsley of violet; and give them to him to eat with sour bread, and give him light ale to drink; and give him as a suppository a tallow candle up his bottom. And do all this, so that you get better.

To mak a man to pyse wele

TAKE and set hym in a fat nakyde, and close hym upe to the hede in newe drafe, as it comyth fro the ale, the space of an owre. Than wache hym in hoot water, and brynge hym in bede, tyl he have wel slepte.

TO MAKE A MAN PISS WELL

Take him, and put him naked in a vat, and cover him up to the head in new dregs that have come from brewing the ale, for an hour long. Then wash him in hot water, and put him to bed until he's slept well.

For man that may not hold his water

Take the clawes of a gete, and bren hem
and make poudre therof, and let the seke
use hit in his potage, a sponful at onus; and he
schal be hol.

FOR A MAN WHO CAN'T STOP WETTING HIMSELF

Take the claws of a goat and burn them, and make
powder from them, and let the sick man use the
powder in his stew, a spoonful at a time; and he'll
get better.

For swellynge of a mannys pyntyll

TAKE lekys with all the fasinges and wassh hem clene and stampe hem small, and frye hem with barowys grece, and make a plaster al aboute the pyntill. *Another for the same.* Take the jus of weybrode and of rybbe and of prymerose, of echone ylych moche, and do therto floure of rye, and late frye hem wel togidere, and make a plaster aboute, and it wyl do awey the ache and the swellynge. *Another for the same.* Take smalache and herbe Robert and herbe Water, selvegrene and red dokke levys, henbane levys; stampe hem and frye hem togiders in barowys grece and in shepys talowe, and make a plaster therto.

FOR THE SWELLING OF A MAN'S PENIS

Take leeks with all the roots and wash them clean, and grind them small and fry them in the fat of a castrated boar, and make a plaster all the way round the penis. *Another for the same problem.* Take the juice of plantain and of the herb rib and of primrose, of each one a like amount, and add rye flour to that, and fry them well together, and make a plaster around the penis, and it will remove the ache and the swelling. *Another for the same problem.* Take wild celery, herb-Robert and woodruff, sengreen, red dock leaves and henbane leaves; grind them and fry them together in the fat of a castrated boar and in sheep's fat, and make a plaster for the problem.

For swellynge of ballokys

Take bene mele and vynegre, and tempere hem well togidere, and make a plaster therof, and ley therto; but lete it come a ny no feer, for it mote be colde. And if thu have gret benys, stampe hem and tempere hem with hony, and make a plaster, and ley to the sore al colde. Also, take rewe and wermode, stampe hem in a morter, and temper hem togidere with hony, and make a colde plaster, and ley therto.

FOR SWOLLEN BOLLOCKS

Take ground beans and vinegar, and blend them well together, and make a plaster from it, and lay it on the swelling; but never let it get close to the fire, because it must be cold. And if you have large beans, grind them and blend them with honey, and make a plaster, and lay it on the sore all cold. Also, take rue and wormwood, grind them in a mortar, and blend them well together and make a cold plaster, and lay that on the swelling.

For bolnyng of pappes

Tak dregges of aysell and virgyn wax, and mak a plaster and lay therto. *Another*. Take jus of lekes and ache and hate brede crommes, and mell tham with warme hony, and do to poudre of comyn, and mak a plaster and lay to.

FOR SWOLLEN BREASTS

Take vinegar dregs and fresh wax, and make a plaster and lay it on the breasts. *Another.* Take the juice of leeks, celery and hot breadcrumbs, and mix them with warm honey, and add cumin powder to that, and make a plaster and lay it on them.

For melk that may noght of the pappis

ANOYNTE the pappis with squyrels grece, and hit wol go out anon. *Item*. Take bene mele and tempere hit with yolkis of eyren and plastre hit aboute, and hit schal voyde the akyng.

FOR MILK TRAPPED IN THE BREAST

Smear the breasts with the fat of a squirrel, and the milk will come out straight away. *Another.* Take ground beans and blend it with egg yolks and plaster it over the breasts, and that'll take away the ache.

If a woman maye not conceive

TAKE the powder of a hartes horne, and lett yt be myxed with a cowes gall. Let a woman kepe it abowt hir, and then let her do the acte of generacion with hir husband, and she shall conceive. *Another for the same.* Take and gyve the woman mares mylke unbeknowen to her. Then let her doe the act of generacion in that ower, and she shall conceave anone by Godes grace.

IF A WOMAN CAN'T GET PREGNANT

Take powder from the horn of a male deer, and mix it with a cow's bile. Let a woman carry this about with her, and then let her have intercourse with her husband, and she'll get pregnant. *Another for the same problem.* Take a mare's milk, and give it to the woman without her knowledge. Then let her have intercourse within an hour, and she'll get pregnant right away, by the grace of God.

For a man that pisseth blod

Tak the erthe that is in a swalwe nest, and drynke it in hot watur.

FOR A MAN WHO'S PISSING BLOOD

Take the soil from a swallow's nest, and drink it
dissolved in hot water.

For vomytyng of blode

Take the tordelys of a got, and make therof poudre, and tak poudre and i handful barly mele, and do hyt in water, and seth hit wel; and wan hyt ys wele sode, caste i sponful of the poudre that ys makyd of the gotys tordelys therynne; and ofte ete therof, and so shal he be hole.

FOR VOMITING BLOOD

Take the turd-pellets of a goat, and make a powder from them, and take the powder and one handful of barley grains, and put them in water, and boil it well; and when this is well boiled, throw in one spoonful of the powder that was made from the goat's pellets; and eat some of it often, and so he'll get better.

For bledyng at the nose

YIF a man blede at the nose, take and ley his ballokkys in vinegre; and take a clowte and wete it wel in vynegre, and than wete wel the place bytwene his browys and al his forhed. And if it be a woman, take and ley hir brestys in vinegre. And it schall staunche anoone ryght.

FOR A NOSEBLEED

If a man is bleeding from his nose, grasp his bollocks and lay them in vinegar; and take a cloth and douse it well in vinegar, and then wet the spot between his eyebrows and all his forehead. And if it's a woman, grasp her breasts and lay them in vinegar. And the nosebleed will stop right away.

To staunche blod

WRYTE thes letters yn levys of parchment and bynd hem bytwyne thy thyes; and yf thou honiyst hyt nought, take and wryte hem in a knyf, and therwith sle a swyn, and the rennyng therof schal be myche the lasse. Thes beth the letters: *p g T P e n o x a g n N m. Item.* Tak the felt of an holde hat and brend to poudere, and leye upon the wounde, and hit wole staunche.

TO STOP BLEEDING

Write these letters on leaves of parchment and bind them between your thighs; and if you don't believe it, go and write them on a knife, and slay a pig with it, and the bleeding from that will be much less than you expect. These are the letters to write: *p g T P e n o x a g n N m. Another.* Take the felt from an old hat and burn it to ashes, and lay that on the wound, and it'll stop bleeding.

To mak the wisage white and softe

TAK fresch grece of a swyne and henne grece and white of an egge half rosted, and do therto a lytill cokill mele, and enoynt the face therwith.

TO MAKE YOUR COMPLEXION WHITE AND SOFT

Take the fresh fat of a pig and hen's fat and the
white of a half-boiled egg, and add a little of
ground corn, and daub your face with it.

For to do a wey frekenes

TAKE the blod of an hare or the blod of bole, and anoynt the face that is frekened, and hit schal destrie hem clene.

TO GET RID OF FRECKLES

Take the blood of a hare or the blood of a bull,
and daub the face that has freckles, and this will
destroy them completely.

For tethe that be yelowe and stynkyng

TAKE sauge and stamp it a litill, put therto twise so muche of salte, and put hit in a past, and bake hit, til hit be brent. Take thanne and make a powder therof, and rubbe thy tethe therwith on the morowe, and hit shall make theym swete of brethe and whyte.

FOR TEETH THAT ARE YELLOW AND STINKING

Take sage and grind it a little, add to it twice the amount of salt, and mix it into a paste, and bake it, till it's burnt. Then take it and make a powder from it, and rub your teeth with it in the morning, and it will make them white and make your breath sweet.

For to doo awey heere

TAKE the seed of nettylles, stamp hit, and temper hit with aysell. First thou must shave hit awey or elles pulle hyt. And thanne hit behoveth the to swete wel with travayle; and when thou art well hote, anoynt the therwith, and thus iij dayes, every day oonys, for it woll do awey the heire.

TO GET RID OF UNWANTED HAIR

Take the seed of nettles, grind it, and blend it with vinegar. First you must shave the hair off or pluck it out. And then you need to work up a good sweat by exercise; and when you're really hot, smear yourself with the mixture. Do this once a day for three days, for this will get rid of the hair.

Another maner medicyne to make heer to growe

TAKE ladanum, and disolve it in puryd hony; and take an herbe that hatte *capillus verginis* (that is to seyn, *maydyn heer*), and stampe hym in a morter of bras, and hony therwith. And when it is smale inowghe, wryng it thurw a canevas, and put therto the ladanum, and set it on the fyre, and lete it boyle or velme but onys, and set it doun and lete it kele. This wil make heere grewe ovyr alle.

ANOTHER KIND OF MEDICINE
TO MAKE HAIR GROW

Take resin of the cistus bush, and dissolve it in purified honey; and take a herb called *capillus virginis* (that is, *maiden hair*), and grind it in a mortar made of brass, with honey in it. And when it's ground down finely enough, strain it through canvas, and add the resin, and set it on the fire, letting it boil or bubble over only once; then take it off the fire and let it cool. This will make hair grow everywhere.

For to destroye wertes in thyn hondes

Tak and bren the clauwes of a got, and drynk
that with som drynke.

TO GET RID OF WARTS ON YOUR HANDS

Take the claws of a goat and burn them, and drink
the remains mixed with a drink.

For the morfu, whit or blak

TAKE an unce of gode vertgrece and another of quykke brymston, and make hem bothe on poudre, als smale as thou mayght; and take two schepus hedus that ben fat, and let hild hem and clene hem, and take oute the breyn, and aftur wasshe hem clene and sethe hem, tyl they be tendre; and than take doun thi vessel, and let hit kele, and gedre the grece that cometh of hem, and temper hit with the poudres, and make oynement therof. Bot let hit come nye no fire, for hit schal be wrowght al cold. And than anoynt the seke therwith, and that schal hele the morfu, be hit whit or blak.

FOR SKIN LESIONS, WHITE OR BLACK, CAUSED BY MORPHOEA

Take one ounce of verdigris and one of natural sulphur, and reduce them both to powder, as small as you can; and take the head of two fat sheep, and have them flayed and cleaned, and take out the brain, and after wash them clean and boil them, until they're tender; and then take the cooking pot from the fire and let it cool, and gather the grease that pours from the heads, and blend it with the powder, and make an ointment from it. But don't let it get close to the fire, as it needs to be prepared while it's cold. And then daub the sick man with it, and it'll heal the lesions, whether they're white or black.

For sausflem

Take uryne of viij dayes old and hete hit up
the fuyr; therwith wassh thy visage, erliche
and late.

FOR A ZITTY FACE

Take urine eight days old and heat it over the fire;
wash your face with it morning and night.

Of diverse diseasys of the toes

ORDEYNE frest that the pacient have large hosyn and schoone, and than mollifie the hardnesse other the callosite with fattnesse of salt bacon every day, leyeng new of this thyng to tenne or twelfe dayes be past. And whan the place is well mollified, take all the nodosite or the callosite with a nedell, and streyne the nedell manyfoolde with a reede threde abought, and lifte the threde and the nedell upward, and kuytt awey all that is lefte up under the nedell, so that, in as moche as thow may, there leve no thyng of that is reysed up with the nedell. And whan it is kut, cautery the roote well and thriftely and enoynte the place with buttur.

OF DIVERSE DISEASES OF THE TOES

First arrange for the patient to have loose stockings and shoes, and then soften the hardness of calluses every day with fat from salted bacon, applying new bacon until ten or twelve days have passed. And when that part of the foot is well softened, pick at the knotty bits and calluses with a needle, and with a red thread tug on the needle many times, and cut away everything lifted up by the needle, so that, as far as you can, there's nothing left of what was raised up with the needle. And when it's cut off, cauterize the exposed flesh properly and daub the wound with butter.

For alle goutes, gode oynement

TAKE an owle and pulle hym and open hym, as thou woldest ete him; and salt him wel and do him in an erthen pot, and ley a tyl theron, and set hit into a hot oven, when men setten in dowe. And when men drawen forth, loke wether he be ynow for to make poudre of, and yif hit be not, let hit stonde, til hit be; and bete hit to poudre and temper hit with bores grece, and anoynt the sore by the fyre.

A GOOD OINTMENT FOR ALL GOUT

Take an owl, and pluck its feathers, and cut it open, as though you were going to eat it; and add plenty of salt, and put it in a china pot, and place a tile on top, and put it into a hot oven, when men are baking dough. And when they take out the dough, check whether the owl is decayed enough to be pulverized, and if not, let it stand until it is. Then beat it into a powder and blend it with fat from a boar, and daub the wound while you're sat by the fire.

Whoso hath stynkende breth or styngende nose

Tᴀᴋ the blake mynte and the jus of rue, of bothe ylyche moche, and do in thy nosetherlys.

WHOEVER HAS STINKING BREATH OR A STINKING NOSE

Take black mint and the juice of rue, in equal amounts, and put it in your nostrils.

For all maner of sore eyen

TAKE and boyle the red snayle that crepyth and sethe hym in watyr, and geder of the grece, and anoynt thyne eyen therwith; or bren hym to powder, and ley the powder to thyne eyen, and it woll make theym hole *et cetera*.

FOR ALL SORTS OF SORE EYES

Take a red creeping snail and boil it and stew it
in water, and gather up the slime, and daub your
eyes with it; or burn it to powder, and put the
powder on your eyes, and it will heal them,
and so on.

For sor in th'ies

STAMPE schepis terdelis with aysel, and smere thy ies ofte.

FOR A SORE IN THE EYES

Grind the turd-pellets of a sheep with vinegar,
and smear your eyes with it repeatedly.

Of the feblenesse and weknes of syghte

A gotis lyvere roostid and spreynt with pouder of pepir; and ete it; and the lycor therof droppid in his eighe. Allso, sethe the lyver and the splene of a goote, and the skemyng thereof, do it in the eighe. Allso, kitt the lyver of a goote and salt it and sethe it in vynegre, and hange the eyghen over the smoke. Allso, distille a water of eufrace, celendoyne, rewe, egremony, fenell and of roosis. Allso, take the gall of an hare and of an eele, and tempere hem with the forsayd water and hony.

FOR FEEBLENESS AND WEAKNESS IN EYESIGHT

Eat a goat's liver, roasted and sprinkled with pepper; also drop the juice from the goat's liver into his eye. Also, boil the goat's liver and spleen, and whatever you skim off the top, put that in the eye. Also, cut a goat's liver and salt it and boil it in vinegar, and let the steam get in your eyes. Also, distil juice from the herbs eyebright, celandine, rue, agrimony, fennel and roses. Also, take the bile of a hare and an eel, and blend them with that juice and with some honey.

*Medicine for pyn or webbe in mannus
eyghe or wommannus.*

Tak water of fenel and of bresewort, and put
it therinne, and drynke chesteloukes smale
ygronde. Othur tak the blod of an hous culvere,
and droppe hit hot in thyn eyghe.

A MEDICINE FOR CLOUDINESS OR CATARACTS IN A MAN'S OR WOMAN'S EYE

Take water infused with fennel and the bruisewort daisy, and put it in the eye, and drink finely ground cabbage stalks. Or else take the blood of one of your pet doves, and drop it in your eyes while it's still warm.

Of the webe in the eye

TAKE the blood of a blak flyen that sitten on hokkes other on comferys that schitith reed dirte, and medele it in thyn hond with spatell, and withinne thre dayes it brekith the webbe. And the blood of an eele and his gall, and the samonys allso, helith such siknes, and the grece of a quale and the fattnesse of an hare, for it brekith the stone in mannys bladder; and a lapwyng and her brayn dryed, and the hoot blood of a swalow, and the poudre of schoo solys brent, and the blood of a grene efte whan the heede and the tayle bene kytt of, for they been venemous.

OF CATARACTS IN THE EYE

Take the blood of a beetle that sits on the
hollyhock or comfrey plant and that shits red dirt,
and stir it by hand using a spatula, and within
three days it'll break up the cataract in your eye.
And the blood and bile of an eel, and of a salmon
too, heal such diseases, as does the fat of a quail
or an hare, for that also breaks up a gallbladder
stone; and so do the dried brain of a lapwing, and
the still warm blood of a swallow, and the ash
from burnt shoe-soles, and the blood of a green
newt, if you cut off the head and the tail, which
are poisonous.

Another good collery

TAKE the gallis of bredis that levith bi ravyn, and tempere therwith the poudre of mirre, aloes, sarcocolle, encense, perles and white corall, of everyche of them lyche moche; but looke that thow ley not ever more corosyves but other while mittygatyves and comfortatyves and mollityves, for ellis thow myghtist thorow violence of corosyves distrie the eyghe.

ANOTHER GOOD EYE-WASH

Take the bile of birds of prey, and blend with it
powder from myrrh, aloe, gum resin, incense,
pearls and white coral, with equal amounts of
each; but be careful not to use ever more corrosive
ingredients, but instead to use more soothing,
comforting and softening ingredients, or else you
might, through the violence of the corrosives,
destroy the person's eye.

For the fallyng yvel

THE ballokes of a bore, ydronke, heleth that same yvel. *Item*. The liquor that cometh out of a wetheres longes heleth that yvel. . . . *Item*. A gerdel of wolvys skyn: were hym, and thou schalt never have hit while thou werist hym. *Item*. Poudre the blod of an hertis herte, and tempere hit with water and drynk hit, and be hol. . . . *Item*. Pouder of shalow donge: gif hit the sike to drynke; hit helpeth hym anon. *Item*. Take a ded mannes hed and wassh it in clene water and stampe hit al to poudre and gif hit the sike to drynke erliche and late, and hit helpeth hym anon.

FOR EPILEPSY

The bollocks of a bore, drunk in a liquid, heal this
disease. *Another.* The liquid that oozes from the
lungs of a ram heals that disease. . . . *Another.* A belt
made from a wolf's skin: wear it, and you'll never
suffer an attack while you're wearing it. *Another.*
Powder the blood from the heart of a hart, and
blend it with water and drink it, and get better. . . .
Another. Powdered dung from the rudd fish: give it
to the sick person to drink; it'll cure him quickly.
Another. Take a dead man's head, wash it in fresh
water, grind it to powder and give it to the sick
person to drink, morning and evening, and it will
soon help him.

For the cold fiver

TAKE iij drops of womans mylke, and mylkes a knaffe childe, and do it in a hen egge that es neche sodyne, and lat him sowpe it for the evell.

FOR FEVER CHILLS

Take three drops of milk from a woman who is breastfeeding a baby boy, and put it inside a soft-boiled hen's egg, and let the sick man snack on that for this disease.

Here begynnyth medecine for the dropesy

WHAN water is betwene the skyn and the flesch, tak schavyng of schepis skynnys or of netis skynnys and seth hem in water, tyl they be thykke as glu; and do it in a cloth and bynd abowte the body.

HERE BEGINS A CURE FOR DROPSY

When you've got water retention underneath
your skin, take shavings from the skin of sheep or
cattle and boil them in water, until they're as thick
as glue; and wrap this in cloth and bind it round
the body.

For to breke the stone

TAKE a coke that is xij moneth olde and
opyn hym, and thou schalt fynde in hys
magh stones. Take and breke thame in a mortur,
and temper the pouder therof and drynk it
with wyne.

TO BREAK UP KIDNEY STONES

Take a twelve-month-old cockerel, split it open, and you'll find stones in its stomach. Take them and crush them in a mortar, and blend the powder with wine, and drink it.

For the flux

TAK a chekene yong, dight hym, tak out the
bowelis, and put in hym good mede wex,
and roste hym and gyf the seke to ete.

FOR DYSENTERY

Take a young chicken, prepare it for eating, take out its innards, and replace them with good wax from meadow flowers, roast it and give it to the sick person to eat.

For a man that is sore ybete

TAK weyhore and boyle it in good feyn ale, and drynk it ferst a morwe and last an evene; and make hym a bed in hot horse dongge, and ley hym therinne.

FOR A MAN WHO'S BEEN PAINFULLY BEATEN

Take cudweed and boil it in fine ale, and drink it
first thing in the morning and last thing at night;
and make the patient a bed in a pile of steaming
horse dung, and lay him in it.

Ife a man have an arowhede or any blade in hym

TAKE the gall of a hare hole and lay to
the hole, and it will drawe it owt withowt
any anguys.

IF A MAN HAS AN ARROWHEAD
OR ANY BLADE STUCK IN HIM

Take all the bile from a hare and lay it on the entry-wound, and it will draw out the arrowhead or blade without any pain.

To save one from sword or gone ore any wepen

WRITE thes words and letters in virgin parchment and carri them aboute you: *ff velle tofetis achætum + zadit + tizadit + zadan abi atit + zadne et ‖ = æd b + abiat + ‖ + ‖ + b x in + d + x x + h + z + o + b + l + eliam + l + ff + m + m + P + v + j.* Yf you be in dought of thes, prove it apon a doge which is all rede.

TO PROTECT YOURSELF FROM A SWORD, GUN OR ANY OTHER WEAPON

Write these words and letters on blank parchment and carry them round with you: *ff velle tofetis achætum + zadit + tizadit + zadan abi atit + zadne et | = æd b + abiat + | + | + b x in + d + x x+ h + z + o + b + l + eliam + l + ff + m + m + P + v + j*. If you doubt this'll work, test it on a dog which is completely red.

For bytynges of an edder

TAKE centory and stampe hit and temper hit with his owne uryne, and gif the seke to drinke; and hit is als god to best as to man.

FOR SNAKE BITES

Take the herb centory and grind it and blend it with the sick man's own urine, and give him the mixture to drink; and it works just as well for an animal as for a person.

That no doge barke at the

Take a byche qwen scho es of sawte and fla hire, and take hire skyne, and make the a payre of gloves therof; and als lange as thou has tham on, schal no doge barke at the.

TO STOP DOGS FROM BARKING AT YOU

Take a bitch dog when she is on heat and flay her, and take her skin, and make yourself a pair of gloves from it; and whenever you wear them, no dog will bark at you.

For bitynge of a wood hounde

TAKE tounge cresses and puliol and sethe hem in water, and drynke it, and it shal caste oute the venym. And if thou may have of the houndys heer, caste it on the wounde and bynde it therto, and it shal heel it.

IF YOU'RE BITTEN BY A RABID DOG

Take garden cress and pennyroyal and boil them
in water, and drink it, and it will drive out the
poison. And if you can get any of the dog's hair,
put it on the wound and tie it round, and that'll
heal the wound.

For man that is wode

TAKE genciane sede and rue, and gyfe hym at drynke with weneger; and schaw hys hede; and take a blake coke and clefe hym in two and lay hym to the hede all hote and bynde it fast. Lete it ly a nyght and a day, and the iijd day lett hym blode in the forhede. It is previd forsoth.

FOR A MAN WHO'S GONE MAD

Take seeds of gentian and rue, and give them to the sick person to drink mixed with vinegar; and shave his head; and take a black cockerel and slice it in half and lay it on the patient's head while it's all hot and tie it there tightly. Leave it there for a night and a day, and on the third day do some bloodletting from his forehead. This is proved to work, truly.

To cause a woman to love hir husband and
to forsake all other menes companye

TAKE the lefte foote of a wollfe behynde, and take owt the marrow of it, and bare it aboute the, and she shall not forsake the.

TO MAKE A WOMAN LOVE HER HUSBAND AND STOP FLIRTING WITH OTHER MEN

Take the rear left foot of a wolf, and remove the bone-marrow from it, and carry it about with you, and your wife will never leave you.

For love

TAKE thi swetyng yn a fayr bason and clene
and afterwarde put hyt yn a wytrial of glas,
and put therto the shavyng of the nedder party
of thy fete and a lytyl of thy oune dong ydryet
at the sune, and put therto a more of valurion.
And take to drynke, whane that ever ye will, and
he schall love the apon the lyght of thyn yene.
And thys ys best experiment to gete love of what
creature that thou wolt. And Y, Gelberte, have
ypreved that ofte tymys, for trewthe.

FOR LOVE

Catch your sweat in a nice clean basin and
afterwards mix it with sulphuric salt, and add to
it some shavings from the back of your feet and
a little of your own dung dried in the sun, and
add a root of the herb valerian. And take a swig
whenever you want, and he'll love you as soon as
he catches your eye. And this is the best proven
method to win love from whomever you want.
And I, Gilbert, have proved this many times,
in truth.

For to be invysybell

TAKE an erthen pote and bore yt full of holys, and put therin a frosh, that ys blake spekelede, and stope yt faste and sete yt in a pysmere hyll, ther many rede pyssmers be, and come agen at the 3d dayes ende, and then take the bonys, and goo to a rynnyng water that renneth, and caste them in, and that bone that gothe ageyn the strem, kepe yt and wynde yt in sylke and closse yt in a rynge, or out of a rynge, and bere yt with the, and thou schalt goo invysebell. Also, yyf thou towche a whoman with the forseyde bone, sche schall folowe thy wyll and be at thi comaundment. *Probatum est.*

TO BE INVISIBLE

Take a china pot and drill it full of holes, and put inside it a black speckled toad, and close it tight and put it on top of an anthill, where red ants live, and come back at the end of the third day, and then take the bones, and go to a stream that is flowing, and cast the bones in, and whichever bone moves in the opposite direction to the stream, keep it and wrap it in silk and enclose it in a ring, or outside a ring, and carry it round with you, and you will be invisible. Also, if you touch a woman with that bone, she'll do your desires and be at your command. *It is proven*.

REFERENCES AND CREDITS

This list gives the shelfmark and folio for the manuscripts from which each remedy is taken. All manuscripts are currently housed in the Bodleian Library, Oxford. The list also identifies who selected and transcribed the recipe:

p. 12: MS Additional A. 106, fol. 274v, Anneli Strutt; p. 14: MS e Musaeo 52, fol. 53r, Anneli Strutt; p. 16: MS Douce 84, fols 42v-43r, Justine Gomes; p. 18: MS Hatton 29, fol. 96r, Daniel Wakelin; p. 20: MS Douce 84, fol. 18r, Daniel Wakelin; p. 22: MS Ashmole 1413, p. 105, Daniel Wakelin; p. 24: MS Laud misc. 553, fol. 25v, Anneli Strutt; p. 26: MS Ashmole 1432, pp. 90-91, Sian Witherden; p. 28: MS Ashmole 1432, p. 92, Sian Witherden; p. 30: MS Hatton 29, fol. 95v, Daniel Wakelin; p. 32: MS Laud misc. 553, f.53r, Daniel Wakelin; p. 34: MS Ashmole 1378, p. 46, Sian Witherden; p. 36: MS Douce 84, fol. 4r, Daniel Wakelin; p. 38: MS Laud misc. 553, fol. 44r, Hannah Bower; p. 40: MS Douce 84, fol. 42v, Justine Gomes; p. 42: MS Laud misc. 553, fol. 40r-v, Paoula Sobanda; p. 44: MS Hatton 29, fol. 92r, Daniel Wakelin; p. 46: MS Laud misc. 553, fol. 26v, Anneli Strutt; p. 48: MS Bodley 483, fol. 10r, Cosima Gillhammer; p. 50: MS Bodley 483, fol. 7v, Cosima Gillhammer; p. 52: MS Douce 84, fol. 40v, Justine Gomes; p. 54: MS Douce 84, fol. 4r, Daniel Wakelin; p. 56: MS Laud misc. 553, fol. 25r, Anneli Strutt; p. 58: MS Laud misc. 553, fol. 45r, Daniel Wakelin; p. 60: MS Bodley 178, fol. 140v, Annaliese Griffiss; p. 62: MS Laud misc. 553, fol. 25v, Hannah Bower; p. 64: MS Radcliffe Trust e. 4, fol. 1v, Anneli Strutt; p. 66: MS Bodley 483, fol. 7r, Cosima Gillhammer; p. 68: MS Douce 84, fol. 7r, Daniel Wakelin; p. 70: MS Bodley 178, fols 67v-68r, Annaliese Griffiss; p. 72: MS Douce 84, fol. 18r, Daniel

Wakelin; p. 74: MS Bodley 178, fols 64v, 65r-v, Annaliese Griffiss; p. 76: MS Bodley 178, fols 65v-66r, Annaliese Griffiss; p. 78: MS Laud misc. 553, fol. 46r, Hannah Bower; p. 80: MS Wood empt. 18, fol. 43v, Daniel Wakelin; p. 82: MS Radcliffe Trust e. 4, fol. 3v, Anneli Strutt; p. 84: MS Additional A. 106, fol. 270r, Anneli Strutt; p. 86: MS Radcliffe Trust e. 4, fol. 4v, Anneli Strutt; p. 88: MS Douce 84, fol. 17v, Daniel Wakelin; p. 90: MS Ashmole 1438, I, p. 71, Daniel Wakelin; p. 92: MS Ashmole 1416, fol. 124v, Paoula Sobanda; p. 94: MS Laud misc. 553, fol. 25v, Anneli Strutt; p. 96: MS Wood empt. 18, fol. 31r, Daniel Wakelin; p. 98: MS Additional B. 60, fol. 50r, Daniel Wakelin; p. 100: MS Additional A. 106, fol. 270v, Anneli Strutt; p. 102: MS Ashmole 1378, p. 47, Sian Witherden; p. 104: MS Ashmole 1447, p. 42, Daniel Wakelin; p. 106: MS e Musaeo 52, fol. 61v, Daniel Wakelin

The remedies were translated by Daniel Wakelin.

We gratefully thank Mr John Griffiths and Mrs Jeanne Griffiths, whose generous benefaction for the Jeremy Griffiths Professorship and Studentship, in memory of their son, supports the classes from which this book emerged.

FURTHER READING

The transcriptions and translations were made with the help of *The Middle English Dictionary,* online at http://quod.lib.umich.edu/m/med/; *The Oxford English Dictionary*, in the full version online at http://www.oed.com/; Tony Hunt, *The Plant Names of Medieval England* (Cambridge: Brewer, 1989); and Juhani Norri's database *Dictionary of Medical Vocabulary in English, 1375-1550: Body Parts, Sicknesses, Instruments, and Medicinal Preparations* (London: Routledge, 2016).

Many collections of remedies were first found by consulting *The Index of Middle English Prose*, general editor A.S.G. Edwards (Cambridge: Brewer, 1984- ongoing). Kari Anne Rand Schmidt, 'The *Index of Middle English Prose* and Late Medieval English Recipes', *English Studies*, 75 (1994), 423-29, analyses the challenges of using *The Index* for studying remedies.

Toni Mount, *Medieval Medicine: Its Mysteries and Science* (Stroud: Amberley, 2016), chapter 6, discusses remedies which might actually have worked. Recent medical research by the 'Ancient Biotics' project is confirming the effectiveness of others, as this video reports: https://youtu.be/mo4K51bQVso [accessed 26 November 2016]. Anne Van Arsdall, 'Challenging the "Eye of Newt" Image of Medieval Medicine', in Barbara S. Bowers, ed., *The Medieval Hospital and Medical Practice* (Aldershot: Ashgate, 2007), pp. 195-205, warns that we should not – as this book guiltily does – focus on the outlandish remedies.

For general introductions to medicine in the fifteenth century, see Faye Getz, *Medicine in the English Middle Ages* (Princeton, NJ: Princeton University Press, 1998), and Carole Rawcliffe, *Medicine and Society in Later Medieval England* (Stroud: Sutton, 1995).

For a linguistic study of remedies and other practical recipes, see Irma Taavitsainen, 'Middle English Recipes: Genre Characteristics, Text Type Features and Underlying Traditions of Writing', *Journal of Historical Pragmatics*, 2 (2001), 85-113, and for a literary study, see Carrie Griffin, 'Reconsidering the Recipe: Materiality, Narrative and Text in Later Medieval Instructional Manuscripts and Collections', in Susan Powell and Emma Cayley, ed., *Manuscripts and Printed Books in Europe, 1350–1550: Packaging, Presentation and Consumption* (Liverpool: Liverpool University Press, 2013), 135-149. The forthcoming Oxford DPhil. of Hannah Bower, one of the transcribers for the present book, will offer a longer study.